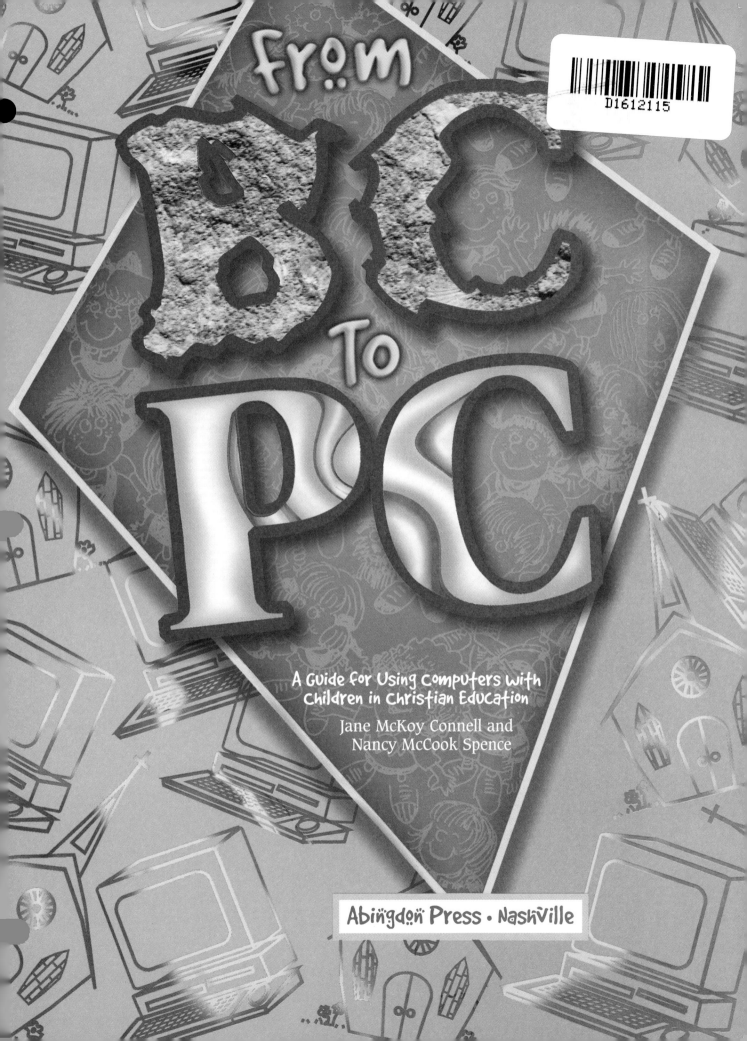

from BC to PC

A Guide for Using Computers with
Children in Christian Education

Jane McKoy Connell and
Nancy McCook Spence

Abingdon Press • Nashville

From BC to PC

ISBN 0-687-07403-7

99 00 01 02 03 04 05 06 07 08 - 10 9 8 7 6 5 4 3 2 1

Special thanks to the children and staff of Roswell United Methodist Church and to Floyd and Tom Connell, Carol Knight, Jeff Barnes, Jimmy Clutter, Tyler Jackson, Delia Halverson, Dr. H. McCreal Chapman, Mr. C. B. McCook, Dr. C. Frank McCook, Dr. Michael Miller, Alison Wright, Marsue Minton, Christel Johnson, Stan and Vicki Rogers, Connie Chaffin, Helen Lauer, Barbara Anderson, Mona Bender, Linda Moe, Sonia Terry and everyone who encouraged us in putting this book together.

About the authors: Jane McKoy Connell and her husband Floyd began teaching children in Sunday school 30 years ago. They are parents to Anna, John, and Tom and have been foster parents for many other children. Nancy McCook Spence, a former school teacher, has been Director of Children's Ministries at Roswell United Methodist Church in Roswell, GA for over 15 years. She is the mother of Tim (wife Marlena) and Linda and has one granddaughter, Serena.

Table of Contents

Appendix Pages:

"Our Story"

"Sunday school is boring."
"It's the same old thing every week." "Do I have to go?" Familiar words? We were hearing them too often with our sophisticated, school age boys and girls. We had children who had been in Sunday school faithfully for years, boys and girls who were experiencing Sunday school for the first time and children who were in week-day Christian schools. We had boys and girls who knew all the major Bible stories and boys and girls who knew no Bible stories.

In 1996, we decided to make some changes in our teaching methods. We felt the use of the computer as a teaching tool would address the needs of many different types of learners in various stages of their Christian growth. We wanted our Christian education program to be challenging, relevant to life, and a means of making creative disciples. We began with one fourth grade class.

The students were studying the life of Jesus using our denominational curriculum. In addition to the usual teaching tools, the boys and girls used CD ROM computers for Bible research and a word processing program to write their own versions of Bible stories. They worked primarily in groups of three. The class decided to create a newspaper that would tell the stories of Jesus' life and would inform readers of a new method for learning in Sunday school. Computers were in! The students printed 90 copies of their paper which they "sold" to members of the congregation. After expenses the boys and girls had $101 which they sent to the Heifer Project (an organization for supplying animals to economically needy persons who pass on the gifts).

Some of the benefits of the project were:

• The children reinforced their learning of the Bible stories by writing them down.

• They shared the Good News with others and had personal contact with other church members.

• They contributed to the Heifer Project.

• They made cooperative decisions in making assignments for writing and publishing and in selecting the project to receive their profits.

• They willingly attended a three hour Sunday school class two weeks before the paper hit the church steps for sale! Attendance increased overall, too.

The students thought the end product of their project was the newspaper. The true end product was the learning that took place in creating the project. That learning helped make better disciples for Jesus Christ.

Since that first project using computers in Sunday school, our program has grown and we use the computers in many varied activities to enrich our curriculum and expand our ability to spread God's word.

In this notebook we will:

- provide a sample Sunday school lesson showing how computers can be used with 4th–6th graders

- illustrate computer activities for 12 major Bible stories

- show activities adaptable to multiple biblical themes

- offer suggestions for various settings when using computers with children

- provide specifications for equipment needed to begin computer teaching/learning in Sunday school

Physical Settings

One Computer

A borrowed lap-top computer can be used to introduce a church to the use of technology with children in Sunday school.

- Teachers can create crossword puzzles (Word Attack) or quizzes to go with a lesson

- Leaders can produce an original slide show (Kid Pix by Brøderbund or PowerPoint-Microsoft Office) presentation to give an introduction to the lesson

- Small groups of children can work together to publish a newsletter relating to the topic for the day

The Computer Center (two or more computers)

We prefer the term "computer center" to "computer lab." The lab terminology has the connotation of a sterile environment with a child and a computer. For us the center suggests a central place for shared learning.

Multiple computers allow more students to work at the same time on the computers. Two to five boys and girls can work together using one computer. The children quickly discover the fastest keyboarder, the technology expert, the creative thinker, etc. An adult or teenager with each group helps the boys and girls stay focused and on task.

Scheduling for the Center

- Computer center teachers study the material for 4th–6th grades each week and devise ways to incorporate the computer with the curriculum. Regular classroom teachers sign up for computer sessions and act as aides for the center teachers.

- By allowing classes to sign up for two consecutive Sundays in the center, they can get closure on projects that may run over the anticipated one session time frame. Projects, reports, etc. can be printed during the week and mailed to participants, thus enhancing interest, and increasing attendance.

- Keeping a log each week of the classes and teachers participating, as well as the lessons and activities used, helps the center teacher with future planning (see sample).

Expanding the base of teachers

- Many people in the congregation have computer skills but do not feel competent to teach children. Bring those members into the computer center as technology resource persons to help students with the use of the computers.

- Many of these resource people discover gifts for teaching of which they were unaware.

- Parents who help in the computer center discover ways to teach, to secure funds for more hardware and software, and become advocates for the ministry.

Computer based teaching and learning is an excellent tool for use in adapting curriculum to the many ways children learn. With the increasing interest in Gardner's theory of multiple intelligences (verbal/linguistic, logical/mathematical, visual/spatial, body/kinesthetic, musical/rhythmic, interpersonal/intrapersonal) teachers are able to use one tool and appeal to students with many different learning styles. Whether it is shared study or individual journaling, students enjoy and reinforce their Sunday school lessons with the computers. They use stories, poetry, original drawings, graphics, and maps to illustrate their understanding of the biblical story. Manipulating graphics, selecting and adding sounds to presentations, thinking through the creative process and presentation layout are techniques that enrich the learning experiences for boys and girls who use computers.

Throughout the teaching process, it is important that each child feel that he/she is a unique child of God who is loved for her/his own individual self. Each person grows in faith at an individual pace and can continue that growth throughout life. The computer is one more tool to aid in that growth.

Before You Begin . . .

Teaching Sunday school using computers is exciting! We hope you will enjoy using this book to enhance your lessons and expand with your own ideas. Most of the activities can be adapted to any Bible lesson, so be creative.

Tips for teachers:

- Share God's love with the students through your warmth and acceptance in the computer center. This is more important than any computer or teaching material.

- Remember that the computer does not teach the children—you do.

- Always have students include their first and last names on all their work.

- Display work outside the center for the congregation to see and send work home with the students.

- Three students per computer is ideal but as many as six children per computer can work.

- In Kid Pix when several groups of children create a slide show, each group can use the same "stamp" head for a character, but can vary clothing. This makes the character recognizable throughout the show.

- Computer software is also sold in "lab packs." If you need more than two copies of the same software, check on this pricing. It's much cheaper in most cases.

- Practice with the software and click on all the buttons to learn the capabilities of the program.

- Tell all adult helpers to keep their hands off the mouse—let the children do everything. Adults are present for encouragement and assistance but not to do the work.

- Have students save their work frequently! This cannot be emphasized enough.

- Decide on a system for naming and saving files before you begin. We use the date, Sunday school hour and group —03299891 (March 29, 1998, 9 o'clock class, group 1). Be consistent and make sure that all helpers use the same system.

After a year of seeing the excitement in our computer center we decided to share our experiences through this book. Please let us know if this is helpful. Also, share with us your ideas for incorporating technology and computers in Christian education settings. Together we can discover exciting and relevant new methods for teaching and learning with children in Christian education.

We want to hear from you! Contact us at: *fconnell@mindspring.com* and *nspence@mindspring.com*

Abraham and Sarah
Scripture: Genesis 12, 13, 17, 18 & 24
Activity: Map Drawing

Tools/Materials Needed:
Bible Land Map
Kid Pix Studio by Brøderbund

Before You Begin:
After studying the story of Abraham's call by God and God's covenant with Abraham and Sarah, students will be ready to show their creativity and understanding of the story by drawing a map of Abraham and Sarah's travels. This activity will allow them to study the scripture and will reinforce their learning. If time permits they might place a small graphic at locations where events took place (example: altar at Shechem)

Directions:
Give each group of students a photocopied map with a horizontal and a vertical line drawn dividing the map into 4 equal parts. This will help students place locations more accurately on their computer drawn map. Also give them a list of the places that should be included on their map. Encourage the students to have fun drawing while they learn the relationships between locations on the map. Keep drawings simple (example: the Great Sea can be drawn as an odd shaped box with a line extending from the bottom for the Nile River.)

Places to be included on map:
(Choose locations important to your studies.)

Ai	Great Sea (Mediterranean Sea)	Persian Gulf
Babylon	Haran (Terah died)	Red Sea
Bethel (tent)	Hebron (altar)	Sea of Galilee
Canaan	Jordan River	Shechem (altar)
Dead Sea	Negeb Desert	Tigris River
Egypt (pharaoh)	Nile River	Ur
Euphrates River	Nineveh	

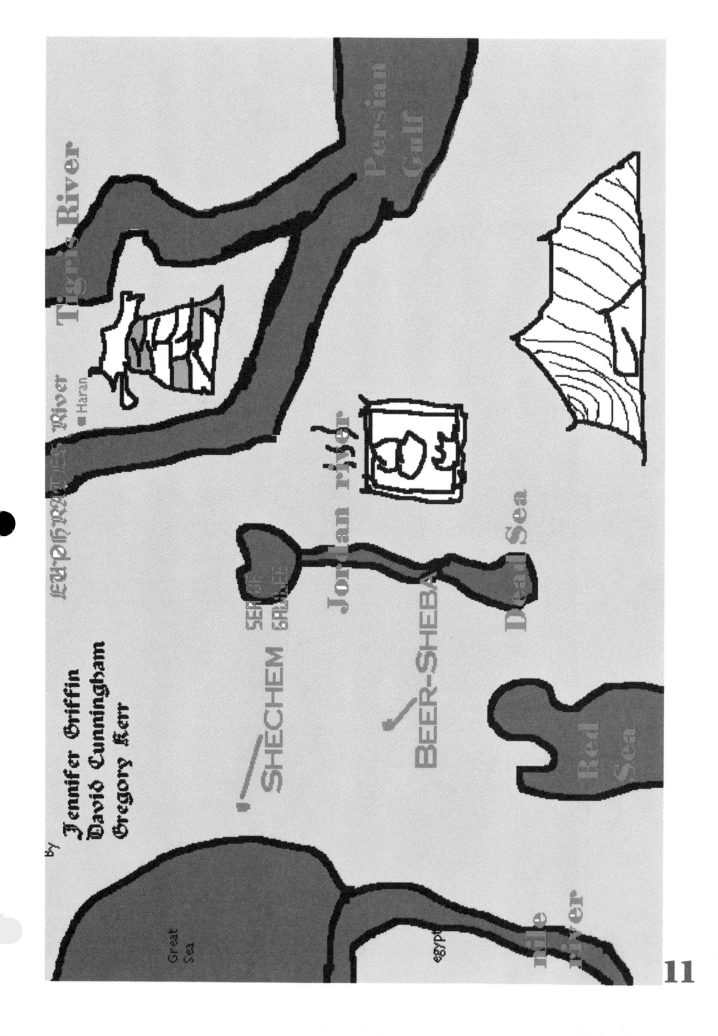

11

Moses

Scripture: Exodus 2 and 3
Activity: Slide Show

Tools/Materials Needed:

Bibles
Kid Pix Studio by Brøderbund

Before You Begin:

After studying the birth of Moses, his call by God, and the episode with the burning bush, students will be ready to show their creativity and understanding of the story by creating a slide show. The show can be expanded as their study of the Exodus progresses. This activity will allow the students to study the scripture, deepen their understanding of the story and will reinforce their learning.

Directions:

Assign each group of students a selection of the scripture to summarize and create slide(s) to express their understanding. After each group has completed their work, slides can be combined to present the story in a slide show. Slides can be created each Sunday for several weeks as you do your study. Invite parents and students to view the completed project together.

Group I—Exodus 2:1-10   Group III—Exodus 3:1-9
Group II—Exodus 2:15-25   Group IV—Exodus 3:10-15

Your Notes:

BURNING BUSH

Kate McGahee, stephanie portis

EXODUS 8: 1-2
THE SECOND OF TEN PLAGUES IN EGYPT

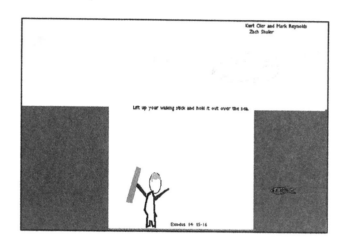

Kurt Oler and Mark Reynolds
Zach Shuler

Lift up your walking stick and hold it out over the sea.

Exodus 14: 15-16

HOLY MOUNTAIN

Katie Martin, Abby Hammond, and Amanda Gillentine

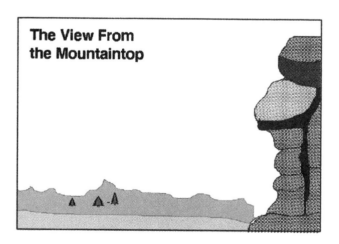

The View From the Mountaintop

Ruth and Naomi

Scripture: Ruth
Activity: Story Door Board

Tools/Materials Needed:
Bible
Print Artist 4.0 by Sierra

Before You Begin:
Prepare first page of story-door board with title of study and scripture references.

Have first page of story-door board open on computer screen when students enter (sample included in appendix).

Directions:
After studying the story of Ruth and Naomi students will enjoy retelling the story in their own words and with pictures. Assign each group of students one chapter of Ruth to review and summarize into four parts. Challenge each group of students to create one story-door board containing four frames for their chapter. Have students add their name(s) to first page (front cover) and save file. Open second page file and tell students to write and illustrate their story, staying within the square frames. Ask them to place their story in sequence so that their first "picture" will appear behind door #1, etc.

After students have completed their work, print both pages. Prepare top sheet (cover) by cutting each square frame on top, bottom and right sides to open "doors." Glue top sheet (cover) to bottom sheet, being careful to leave squares without glue.

Your Notes:

The Story of Ruth and Naomi

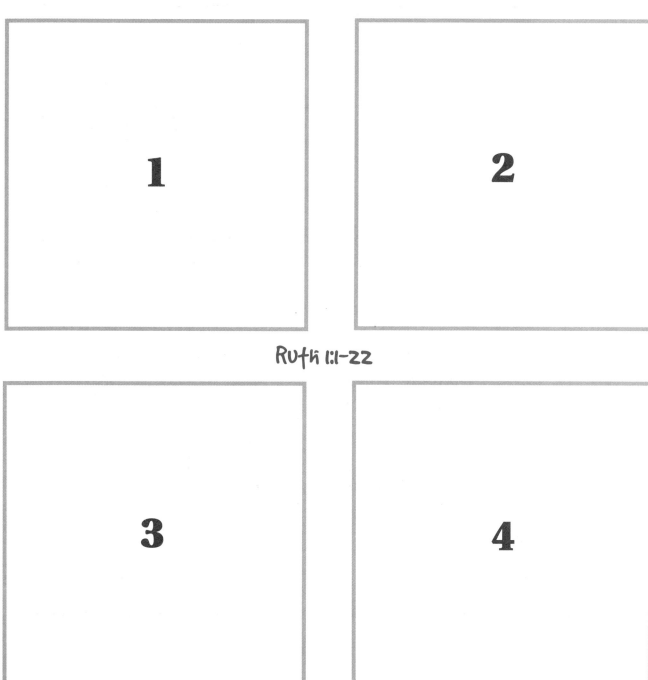

Ruth 1:1-22

As told by: Student Name(s)

There was a famine in Bethlehem.

Elimelech & Naomi & Mahlon & Chilion

move to the land of Moab.

Elimelech died.

Mahlon and Chilion marry Ruth and Orpah. Mahlon & Chilion die.

Ruth

Orpah

Naomi encourages Ruth and Orpah to return to their families because she (Naomi) is going to return to her homeland.

Ruth stays with Naomi saying "for where you go, I will go and where you lodge, I will lodge. Your people shall be my people, and your God, my God.

Orpah stays in her homeland.

David and Goliath
(Or any favorite Bible story)

Scripture: 1 Samuel 17:4-50

Activity: Story Books

Tools/Materials Needed:

Bibles

Storybook Weaver by MECC

Before You Begin:

List selected Bible stories that you have studied along with
Scripture references. Let each group choose one favorite story to
retell in their own words as they remember it.

Directions:

Allow students time to discuss and make notes of what they remember of
their story to organize their thoughts. Give students an overview of how
to use Storybook Weaver. Tell them to type in their story first—dividing
text into pages that they wish to illustrate. *Spelling and pronunciation are
not the primary focus of the book—book is unedited by teachers.* After
typing is complete, have students illustrate each page. (Biblical graphics
in Storybook Weaver do not exist so encourage students to use symbolic
graphics where needed.)

Your Notes:

A long time a go there was a relly tall man his name was goliah. he was in the army. he would ask any body to fight him.

One day a boy name David was going to fight him. He only had a sling shot. He knew God was with him. So he challenged him.

David hit him right above the nose and killed Goliah. So Goliah's team gave up.

God Called Jeremiah and Other Prophets

Scripture: Jeremiah 1:1-10
Activity: Design a Bookmark

Tools/Materials Needed:

Bible
Print Artist 4.0 by Sierra

Before You Begin:

Open Print Artist—Craft—New—Office—Bookmark, Office—OK. For this activity you will need to click on and delete everything except rectangle shape. Click on rectangle—go to Color in top menu bar—choose Customize—choose Face—select Color—choose Face Outline—choose Black—OK. **Save this as a new file so that you have outline for bookmarks and will not have to repeat these steps again.**

Directions:

After students have completed their study of how God called the prophets, allow them to design their own bookmarks depicting Jeremiah and one other favorite prophet. *We focused on Jeremiah because of his being called as a youth.* Ask students to include: 1. the prophet's name, 2. where the prophet was when God called, 3. how the prophet responded to God's call, 4. what God called the prophet to do, 5. one unique fact about the prophet, and 6. student's first and last name. Print on cardstock paper, laminate and cut. (Simple directions for using Print Artist are included in appendix.)

Your Notes:

Jeremiah

Jeremiah was just a boy when God called him to be a prophet.

This book is being read by: Tara Holder

Jeremiah thought he was too young and must have been afraid. God told him to go and that He would be with him.

RUMC 5th Grade Sunday School

God called Jeremiah as a boy.

Joseph Brown
October 14, 1997

NOW THE WORD OF THE LORD CAME TO ME SAYING, "BEFORE I FORMED YOU IN THE WOMB I KNEW YOU, AND BEFORE YOU WERE BORN I CONSECRATED YOU; I HAVE APPOINTED YOU A PROPHET TO THE NATIONS."

JEREMIAH 1:4-5

Jonah

Scripture: Jonah
Activity: Teacher-Generated Slide Show and Student Newspaper

Tools/Materials Needed:

Bibles
Kid Pix Studio
Microsoft Word or any word-processing software

Before You Begin:

Prepare a slide show to present the lesson about Jonah and how he was called by God. This can be done in Kid Pix, Microsoft Power Point or any other slide presentation software.

Directions:

Write question "Who Is Called by God?" on the board. Allow students to write their general and specific responses (such as pastors, church workers, Sunday school teachers) on board. Discuss how we are all called by God and encourage each student to write his/her name on board also.

Call students' attention to the computer screen where they can watch the teacher-generated slide show of the story of Jonah. Include (as last slide) a present day situation, and lead discussion as to how they could be called by God in this situation.

Next, have students list different parts of a newspaper with the idea of writing their own. Sports, want ads, front page news, and comics are just a few of the possible responses. Allow students to select a group in which to work and then choose which part of the paper their group would like to write.

If short of time, teacher can format set-up, print and mail to students mid-week. Students as well as parents will be pleased to see their final product.

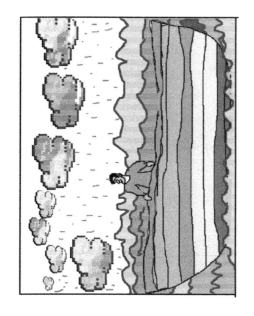

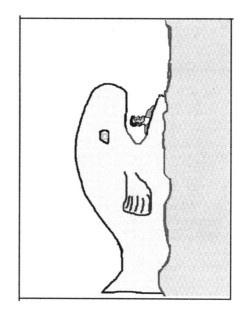

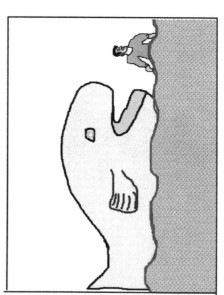

Who Is Called By God?
Teacher generated slide show
Kid Pix
Script voiced in

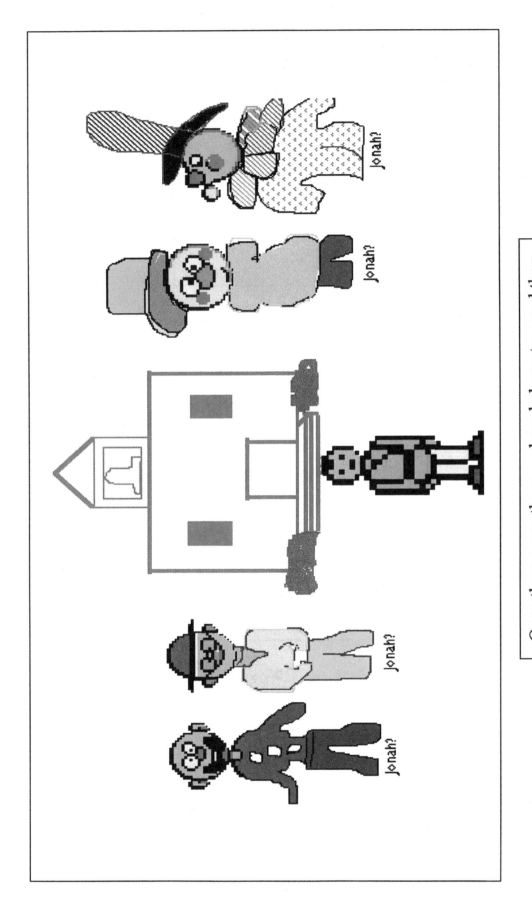

Once there were these real cool characters and then this "kind of weird" guy came to town... Who is called by God in this picture?

Who Is Called By God?

Volume 1 Issue 1   **About 721 B.C.**

MAN NAMED JONAH - SWALLOWED BY BIG FISH

Jonah's Lesson
by Ashley Henke
Matt Lawhorn

Jonah was ordered by God to preach to the enemies. He made the decision not to do this. He and his crew got on a boat and sailed in the opposite direction of where he was to preach. Soon a big storm came. His crew prayed to their gods, but there was no response. Jonah was thrown overboard and swallowed by a big fish. Then the waters were calm again. Then he prayed to God and God heard his prayer. Then the fish threw him up on dry land. He learned his lesson.

Jonah says to his crew, "Throw me overboard."

by: Matt Merritt & Brian Young

Sports

BASKETBALL

Last night the Jesus Jungle Cats crushed the Jonah Jackals in an enormous 104 to 93 lead. The Jungle cats have now officially become the winners of the GBA (Gods Basketball Association) National Championship Playoffs World Tournament. The player of the playoffs was Saul with a triple double in the last half of the last game.
Chris "Pony" Duggan
& Kevin Young

TRACK

At Monday's 20K it was a very close race. It was God and Satan battling it out all of the five grueling hours. But finally, after the race ended, God defeated Satan in an amazingly close photo finish.

Jesus' Birth

Scripture: Luke 1:5–2:20
Activity: Story Box

Tools/Materials Needed:

Bibles
Print Artist 4.0 by Sierra

Before You Begin:

In Print Artist 4.0 choose Craft—Event—Babyshower2, Gift Box—delete yellow rectangles by clicking on *edge* of color and delete—highlight squares—Color—Customize—make Face white and Face Outline black (**repeat for all squares**). Do the same for the two box top flaps. Highlight all remaining graphics and delete. **Save file (boxplain.crf).** Next time you will have box outline ready and there will be no need to repeat the deleting steps. Sample box is included in appendix.

Assign scripture selections for each group. A sample assignment sheet is included in the appendix. Have boxplain.crf file open on each screen when students arrive.

Directions:

After studying the story of Zachariah's visit from Gabriel (Luke 1:5-25), Mary's visit from Gabriel (Luke 1:26-38), Mary's visit to Elizabeth (Luke 1:39-56), the birth of John the Baptist (Luke 1:57-80), Mary and Joseph's journey to Bethlehem, Jesus' birth (Luke 2:1-7), visit from the shepherds (Luke 2:8-20), etc., students will be ready to retell the story in their own words on a story box.

Give each group of students a selection of scripture to review and summarize in their own words. Tell students to insert graphics and text to tell their part of the Christmas story on the sides of the story box. Remind students that some text and graphics will need to be turned with the circular arrow in order for graphic or text to show right-side-up when box is assembled. The **circular arrow** (or turning arrow) is obtained by placing cursor over small black square on the sizing frame. Make sure each group includes the scripture reference on top and students' first and last names on bottom.

Boxes can be printed on copy paper and laminated or printed on card stock and will still fold properly. These make a nice gift for a younger class to use to learn the sequence of the Christmas story.

There are limited numbers of Christian graphics in Print Artist. You find them under the categories of religion, Christ, Christian, Christmas, and Bible. You can copy or scan many graphics from other programs to your desktop paint program (have your graphic on the screen—click on the graphic—go to Edit—select all—Copy) and then go to your desktop paint program (go to Edit-Paste). Your graphic will appear for you to make changes in color and design of the graphic. You then reverse the process by clicking on the revised graphic (go to Edit—copy). In Print Artist— open new sign—(go to Edit—paste). At this point Print Artist will require you to name the graphic and save it as a bitmap file.

Your Notes:

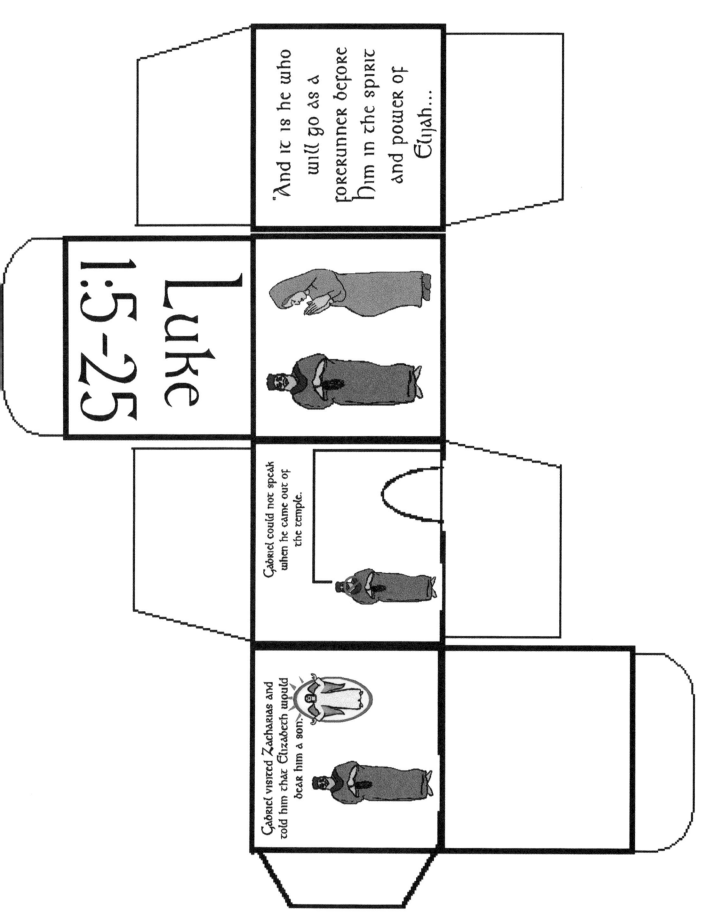

'And it is he who will go as a forerunner before Him in the spirit and power of Elijah...

Luke 1:5-25

Gabriel could not speak when he came out of the temple.

Gabriel visited Zacharias and told him that Elizabeth would bear him a son.

28

Lesson 8

Calling of the 12 Disciples

Scripture: Matthew 4:18-22 & 10:1-4, Mark 3:13-19, Luke 6:12-16
Activity: Invitations

Tools/Materials Needed:

Bible
Print Artist 4.0 by Sierra

Before You Begin:

Because there is little known about some of the disciples, research names, professions, hometown, etc. of each disciple. Have resource books and previous lesson materials about disciples on hand for students to use. (A summary of some facts or beliefs regarding disciples is included in appendix.) Make word-find board and letters (directions included in the appendix). Arrange letters on word-find board so that all 12 disciples are included as well as other familiar names from Bible. *Make sure that you have not spelled any inappropriate words by accident.*

Directions:

As students gather, have them work as one group to find names of disciples on word-find board. Encourage students to call out any names that they see regardless if name is a disciple or not. Make a list on the board of all names called out. Discuss disciples and their call according to your Sunday school material. Correct list on board to include only names of disciples: Simon Peter, Andrew, James, John, Phillip, Bartholomew, Matthew, Thomas, James, Simon, Judas, and Judas Iscariot. Assign three disciples to each group to research and find as many facts as possible. Read scripture together allowing students to identify their disciples in each scripture reference.

Have students open Print Artist—choose Card—New—1/4 fold—OK—Event—Party Invitation—OK. Have students click on and delete each part of front and inside so that they can see how layers are built to make a card. *(There are four sides—front, inside left, inside right and back; you select the side by either clicking on the **shadow** or small triangle outline.)* Instruct students to pretend they are designing an invitation for their disciple(s) from Jesus to come and follow Him. Ask them to include name(s) of the disciple(s) on the front of invitation. Encourage them to be creative and include as many facts regarding disciple(s) as they can find. Display their work where others can view it! *Appendix includes additional card for display.*

29

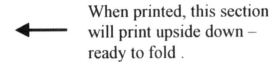

When printed, this section will print upside down – ready to fold .

Simon - also called Simon Peter -was a fisherman and his brother is Andrew.

They were called by Jesus when they were out fishing. They left their nets immediately and followed Jesus.

Peter was the one who denied Jesus three times.

megan scherer

Jesus said to Simon Peter and Andrew..."Follow Me, and I will make you fishers of men."

Jesus Heals

Scripture: Matthew 4:23-26, 8:14-17, 9:1-8
Activity: Get Well Cards, Thanksgiving Box, Prayer Pocket

Tools/Materials Needed:

Bible
Print Artist 4.0 by Sierra

Before You Begin:

In Print Artist 4.0 go to Crafts, New, Categories—occasion, Layouts—valentine envelope, OK, click on & delete all graphics. Click on outline—place "hand" on top and move to side. Click on & delete rectangular shape. Click on outline—place "hand" on top and move back to center. Save file by going to Save As—name file cardblnk.crf—save.

Directions:

After studying the scriptures of Jesus' healing the sick and lame have students make get well cards for hospitalized church members. Explain to students that we can share God's love in many ways—cards being one of those ways. Have blank copy of card open on computer as students enter. Allow students to design get well cards on blank card form by inserting text and graphics. Save card with a different name and then highlight and delete everything except outline form. Have students design front (address side) of card with name and address as well as return address. Print on card stock paper, flip paper and print other side of card on reverse side of paper. Cut out and fold.

If time permits include prayer pocket and thanksgiving box in this lesson. Examples and directions are found in the appendix.

Your Notes:

Roswell United Methodist
814 Mimosa Blvd.
Roswell, GA 30075

Mrs. Sara Thompson
2456 Brown Street
Roswell, GA 30076

32

Get well soon!
We miss you
at church.

RUMC
4th Grade Sunday School

Parables

Scripture: Matthew 13
Activity: Rebus

Tools/Materials Needed:

Bibles
Print Artist 4.0 by Sierra

Before You Begin:

After completing your study on how Jesus taught using parables, allow students to retell the story using pictures and words in a rebus (using pictures in place of words in a phrase). Students can choose any parable you have studied or choose to illustrate Jesus' explanation for the use of parables in teaching.

Directions:

Have a blank screen in Print Artist open on each computer. Tell students to read their scripture and discuss which words they will be able to replace with a picture (graphic).

Allow students to type in their complete scripture, size it small, and place it at the bottom of their page. Next have them type in words (or phrase) that will not be in picture form and place them on the page and insert graphics on the page in separate steps. *Example: From top menu— choose Insert—Text—type in "And he spoke many . . . as he sowed, some."—OK—place it on the page. Choose Insert—Graphic—find a picture of seed—OK—and place it on the page. Choose Insert—Text—type in "fell beside the road..., etc.*

Your Notes:

And he spoke many things to them in parables, sayhing, "Behold the sower went out to sow; and as he sowed, some

 fell beside the road, and the

came and them up.

And others fell upon the rocky places, where they did not have much  and immediately they sprang

because they had no depth of  . But when the had risen, they were

 and because they had no  they withered away.

And He spoke many things to them in parables, saying, "Behold, the sower went out to sow; and as the sowed, some seeds fell beside the road, and the birds came and ate them up. "And others fell upon the rocky places, where they did not have much soil; and immediately they sprang up, because they had no depth of soil. "But when the sun had risen, they were scorched; and because they had no root, they withered away.   Matthew 13:3-6

Jesus and the Children

Scripture: Mark 10:13-16
Activity: Write Your Own Book

Tools/Materials Needed:

Bible
Print Artist 4.0 by Sierra

Before You Begin:

Refer to blank 8-page booklet in appendix and either scan image or draw booklet form in Print Artist. To draw booklet form: Open Print Artist—Sign—New—Blank—11 x 8 1/2 (US Letter)—OK—Insert—Basic Shape—Line, Thin. Move cursor over small square at end of frame until you see the two-sided arrow, click and stretch line across page horizontally, keeping it centered on the page. *Again go to Insert—Basic Shape—Line, Thin—OK. Move cursor over square at right end until cursor becomes a circular arrow, click and turn line vertically, stretch line across page vertically. Move cursor until you see the **hand**, click and **move** vertical line* to intersect with horizontal line at center point of page. Repeat italicized steps twice more to draw a total of three vertical lines, dividing the page vertically into four equal sections. Go to Insert—Text—type "Page 2"—OK. Place cursor over corner square until two-sided arrow appears. Move frame inward so that font (type) becomes very small. Move cursor until you see hand again and then move "Page 2" to lower left section. Repeat page numbering for each section, turning text upside down for pages 6, 7 and 8 so students can visualize the direction that text should be placed on each page. Save file!

Directions:

Following the study of Jesus' life and ministry, ask students to retell the story of how Jesus wanted the children to be allowed to come to Him. Have the blank 8-page booklet form on computer screen and ask students to type their title and their first and last names on page 1 of booklet. Instruct them to type their text on consecutive pages **being careful to notice page numbering.** They may prefer to use graphics as well as words to retell the story.

Print, cut on broken line in center of page and fold according to directions found in appendix.

They Are Our Future

by Lizzie Comery

Jesus was preaching to his people while children came to him.

Page 2

The deciples said no and shewed them away.

Page 3

Jesus said no! Bring them to me they are the future.

Page 4

The children came to the lord.

Page 5

Jesus held them in his arms.

Page 6

Jesus told the people that the children must believe.

Page 7

If the children dont believe then there will be no heaven for them.

Page 8

Easter

Scripture: Luke 24
Activity: Expressive Art

Tools/Materials Needed:

Kid Pix Studio by Brøderbund

Before You Begin:

After studying the Easter scripture and discussing students' thoughts and feelings, they will be ready to "draw and paint" pictures of what they know and feel. You may want to draw and paint a picture to show as an example.

Directions:

Have a blank screen in Kid Pix open and ready at each computer. Demonstrate to the group how they can draw using the pencil, line, square and circle. Also show them how to paint with brush icon and paint-can icon, choosing color and texture from charts at bottom of screen. The eraser allows them to change parts of the drawing without having to start over. Remember to save often. The little man's face can undo the last step (last step only!) without affecting their drawing. Explain how to use the medicine dropper to match colors if they want to repeat a color and can't remember which color was used earlier.

Reminder: Any area must be sealed off (outline **completely closed** or connected) to paint that area or the entire screen will be painted; if this happens use undo before beginning any other step.

Your Notes:

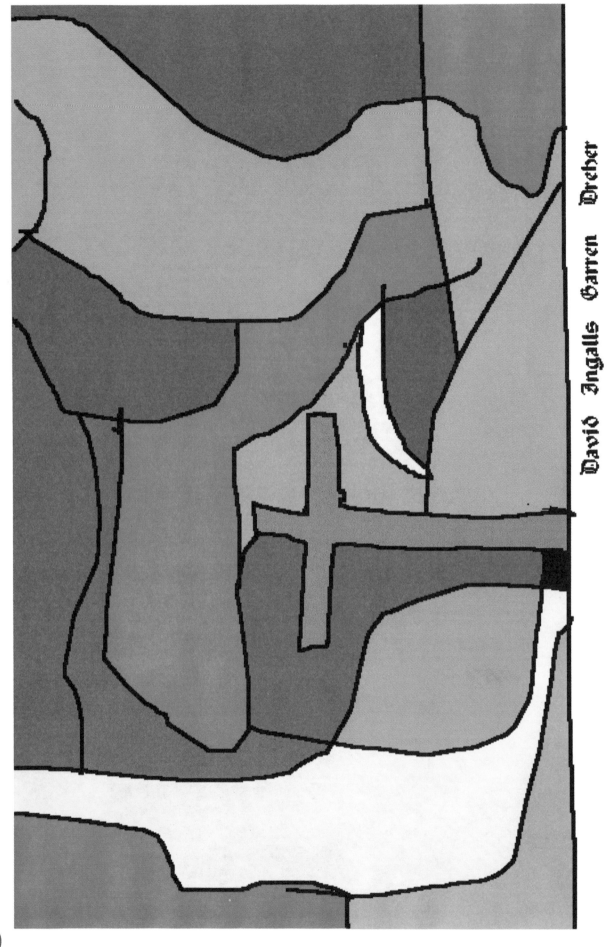

David Ingalls Garren Dreher

40

What Equipment is Needed?

"Technology is changing rapidly. We recommend new, state-of-the-art equipment if possible. Below are the minimum suggestions if you are purchasing equipment. The activities in this manual were created using the following types of equipment."

Computer

- Pentium 120 120MHz or greater (MMX enable Pentium or a Pentium II processor would be preferred since most applications are multi-media)

- 16M Ram, but 32M or more preferred (since most applications used are graphics intensive, this makes things much faster)

- 1.2GB Hard drive or greater (the applications used have LOTS of graphics files with them)

- 15" color Monitor (larger color monitors, like a 17" are useful if you have three or more children sharing the same computer or even a 19" if you plan to use it to show lesson slide shows to entire group)

- 1-2M Vram (video ram) (if you are going to be working with pictures and a larger monitor, you may require 4M of Vram)

- Mouse or Trackball

- Windows 95 Operating System

Printers

- Any color inkjet printer on the market today will do well. Some optional features to look for that may be beneficial to you are:

- Separate black and color ink holders. This will lessen your operating costs if you print primarily in black and white.

- Speed...the faster the printer, the less waiting

Some additional items that may be beneficial to you, but are in no way necessary are:

- Network Cards—If you have network cards, you will be able to connect the computers together and share files and printers. This is really a splurge area.

- A modem and Internet connectivity— With a connection to the internet, you will be able to send e-mail to other church groups, look at Web pages from other churches, etc. Any modem will be sufficient for this use. Most computers come with modems today.

Kid Pix Studio Directions

Complete directions are included with the software. The following is a brief summary to get you started.

Choose File
Choose New

Pencil—draw with the pencil

Line—draw with the line (press and hold the shift key while drawing to obtain a straight line.)

Shapes—draw with the shapes

Paint bucket—Fills in **closed** area with color from the color bar or pattern from the pattern bar

Mixer—produces special effects

Eraser—erases (you can choose the size of the erasure)

Man's happy face—undoes the last action you performed.

A—letter stamps

Typewriter—types in text (choose font (type style) from bottom of screen)

Stamp—choose different stamps from stamp set at the bottom of screen. Additional stamp sets are found under Goodies in the drop down menu (menu at top of screen). When class is preparing a slide show, we have them use the same stamp for main character's face in order to be consistent throughout slide show.

Truck—allows you to move sections of picture. Bar at bottom of screen gives you choices of size of moving box or magnet allows you to draw around section to be moved. Caution: you move everything within the moving box including background and you replace (or cover over) everything beneath area where you paste selection.

Medicine dropper—identifies color you used previously by placing dropper point on color in question and the matching color appears in top rectangle of color chart.

Save each slide as an individual picture through *file save picture*. Choose *slide show* to insert pictures in order. Click on slide icon at lower left corner of truck to insert first slide. *Music note icon* will allow you to add sound effects or record voices. Lower right icon will give options for transitioning between slides.

Storybook Weaver Directions

Complete directions are included with the software. The following is a brief summary to get you started.

Open Storybook Weaver

Choose—*open book* below lamp to write a story
open book on chair to read a story
copier to print a story
door to exit program

New

Choose—*top icon* to enter title
2nd icon to enter author's name
3rd icon to add comments
4th icon to add border
5th icon to change text color
6th icon to add music

At bottom click on right arrow

Choose—*top icon* to select
background—(upper and lower background)
category: scenery, patterns or color
2nd icon to add objects—category: adults, animals, etc.
3rd icon to color object—highlight object—color choices appear choose color 1 or color 2 and your choice of color
4th icon to add sound effects
5th icon to add music
6th icon to spell name of highlighted object
7th icon to reorder highlighted object (place it in front or behind another object)

8th icon to enlarge highlighted object
9th icon to shrink highlighted object
10th icon flips highlighted object's direction
11th icon edits highlighted object (additional screen of options will appear)

Place cursor in lower section to type story.

43

Print Artist Directions

Complete directions are included with the software. The following is a brief summary to get you started.

Open Print Artist
Choose Document Type
Choose Open if document already exists or New if you are creating a document

Text:

From drop down menu choose insert—text.
Text box will appear. Type in text. OK
Text will be selected (box around it) on page.

To add color:
While text is still selected—go to the C button.
From the color pallet you can choose a single color *or*
Choose customize
You can then choose background, background outline, face or face outline and select a color from the color pallet.

To add special effects to text:
While text is still selected—go to the E button.
Choose special effect you wish to use
Then go to the C (color) button while text is still selected
Choose colors (Surface List—if word is bold you are able to change that color, if word is not bold you cannot change color)

To shape text:
While text is still selected—go to Shape in drop down menu or the shape button just below
Choose shape—experiment with these. (Word art pictures can be made this way)

Graphics:

Graphics work basically the same as text.
From drop down menu choose insert—graphic.
Graphic box will appear. Type in name or category of graphic in Type Search Text.
Click on graphic name in *lower* graphic box and scroll down list to find your choice of graphic.

Graphic will be selected (box around it) on page. While graphic is selected click on C in drop down menu. Choose customize. From the Surface List you can change any color that is darkened. If you wish to change a graphic—double click on graphic when "hand" appears.

GROUP ASSIGNMENT FORM

GROUP I

Scripture

Assignment

GROUP II

Scripture

Assignment

GROUP III

Scripture

Assignment

GROUP IV

Scripture

Assignment

Use this form to insure that each group understands its assignment and can work independently.

Computer Center Sign-In
Children's Department

Please record each person who is present in the center this week.

Date _____

Sunday School Class _____

Teachers Present _____

Computer Center Facilitators Present _____

_____

Students Present:

_____   _____

_____   _____

_____   _____

_____   _____

_____   _____

_____   _____

_____   _____

_____   _____

_____   _____

_____   _____

_____   _____

_____   _____

Computer Center Weekly Lessons
Children's Department

Date _____

Class (Grade and Time) _____

Lesson Topic _____

Files saved as: _____

Summary of Lesson (what we did)

Evaluation of lesson (how it went)

Litany of Praise

Give Thanks to the Lord for all the wondrous things He has done. His name endures forever.

With wisdom, *God made the heavens and built the earth on deep waters*
Every creature, great and small, every magnificent rainbow and
the empty tomb are the work of our Lord's fingers.

Open my eyes that I may behold the wonders You have made.

With love, *God created the sun to rule over the day, and the moon and stars to keep watch at night.*
Carefully, The Lord forms each human to have unique ideas, thoughts and emotions.

Open my eyes that I may behold the wonders You have made.

With power, God inspired people to communicate with one another and share
The Story through oral tradition, the printed page and now the mystery of
multimedia.

Open my eyes that I may behold the wonders You have made.

Our God is the Master of everything. The God over all nature and over all
technology.
Lord of the gentlest whisper and of the World Wide Web.
Orchestrator of the seas and of the CD ROM.

Open my eyes that I may behold the wonders You have made.

Lord we pray that You would help us to appreciate the gifts of technology
that You have inspired and use them to give glory to Your name.

Give thanks to the mightiest of all lords, His love is eternal.

Excerpts from Psalm 136

Jennifer Higgins, 1997

Story Door Board

In Print Artist choose Sign, New, Insert, Basic Shape, Square Frame. Change color of square frame to black. Place square frame on page and while it is still selected—choose Edit, Copy and then Edit, Paste. Place 4 squares on page and then choose Object, Group. Save file with two separate names, one for cover page and one for second page.

Insert Title Here

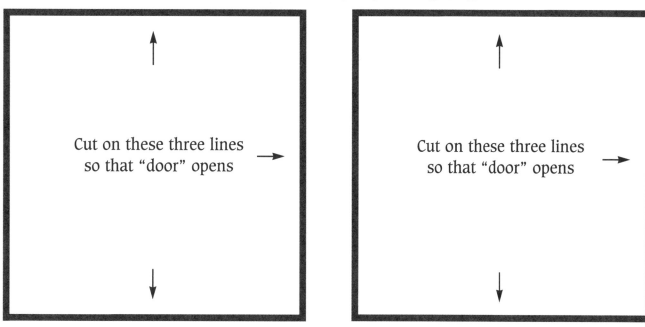

Insert Scripture Reference Here

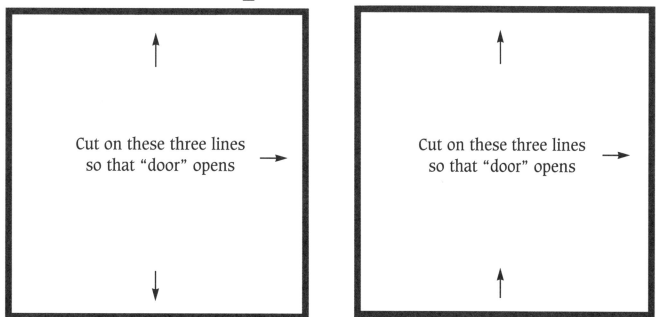

Insert Student Names Here

Story Door Board

(Second Sheet)

In Print Artist have students insert text and graphics to summarize their lesson in these four squares. After printing and cutting—glue this sheet under top sheet being careful to avoid gluing in square areas.

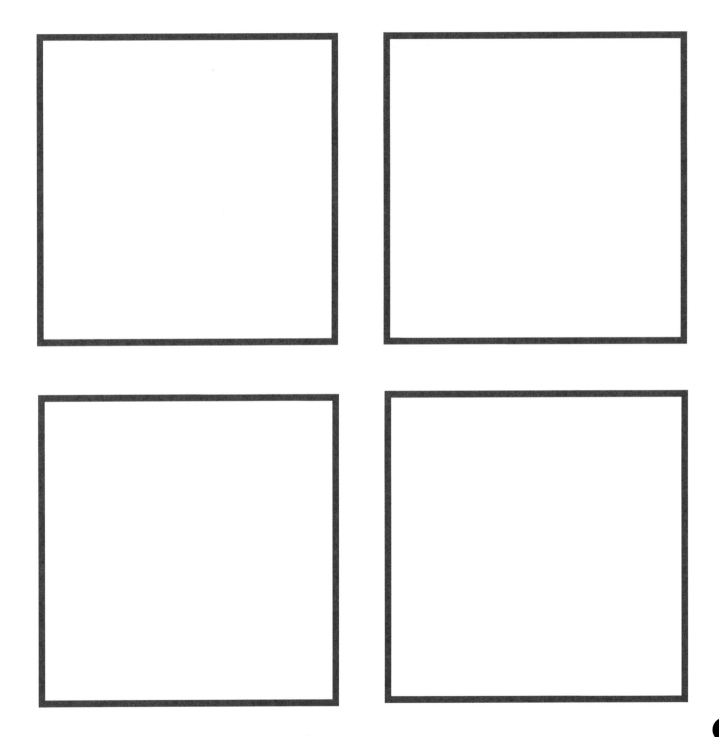

Word Find Board

Cut a piece of plywood (or lightest weight wood you can find) to measure 31" x 36". Place cup hooks—11 across and 14 down at approximately 21/2" intervals.

Print letters (sample included in appendix), laminate and cut out. Punch hole in top center of each letter. These will last and can be used over and over again. This is an excellent *group* activity and a good way to introduce a lesson.

Tools/Materials Needed:

Plywood or other light weight wood
Cup hooks

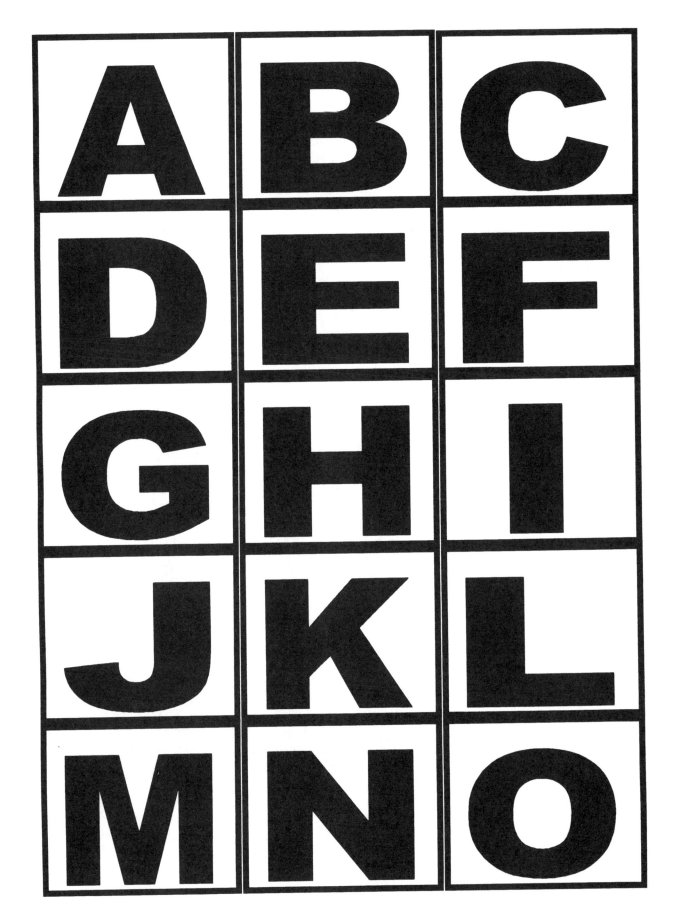

P	Q	R
S	T U	U
V	W	X
Y	Z	A
E	I	O

These facts or beliefs are included for the teacher's use. Select what you think is appropriate for your students.

Simon—also called Simon Peter, Peter, brother of Andrew; fisherman; was one of first four to be called by Jesus; left his nets immediately and went with Jesus; told the story of Christ to the Gentiles; Jesus healed Peter's mother-in-law; first to acknowledge that Jesus was The Messiah; referred to as the rock; denied Jesus three times.

Andrew—fisherman, brother of Simon Peter, one of first four to be called by Jesus; introduced Peter to Jesus; stayed in Jerusalem after resurrection.

James—James the Great, with his brother John called "Sons of Thunder;" one of the closest to Jesus; older brother of John; fisherman; son of Zebedee; was one of first four to be called by Jesus; left his fishing nets immediately and followed Jesus; was with Jesus when Peter's mother-in-law was healed; was with Jesus when Jairus' daughter was raised.

John—one of first four to be called by Jesus; referred to as the disciple "whom Jesus loved;" a fisherman; left his nets immediately and followed Jesus; with his brother James was called "Sons of Thunder;" son of Zebedee.

Philip—introduced his friend Bartholomew to Jesus.

Bartholomew—also known as Nathanael; friend of Philip; an Israelite.

Matthew—also known as Levi; stayed in Judea after Jesus' resurrection; was believed to be well educated; was a despised tax collector; may have written Matthew, one of the four Gospels.

Thomas—known as "the doubter," also known as Didymus (the twin); had to see the nail holes in Jesus' hands to believe.

James the son of Alphaeus—also known as James the Lesser (younger one)

Simon—the Zealot, was with Jesus after the resurrection

Judas—also called Jude, Thaddaeus, Lebbaeus; the son of James; fisherman in Galilee; may have been the head of the Jerusalem church succeeding James.

Judas Iscariot—betrayer of Jesus; treasurer of the group; hanged himself after betraying Jesus.

And He is inviting...

to be His
disciples.

Jesus invited:

James,
Thomas,
Judas Iscariot,
Peter, Philip,
Bartholomew,
Matthew,
Andrew,
Simon Peter,
James, John,

cut out this
center
section and
place
mirror
behind

to be His disciple too!

Draw in Print Artist using basic shapes and lines.
Trim box top and bottom around outside lines.
Fold all solid lines toward wrong side.
Cut designated lines (←Cut these two lines→) – stopping at inside square.
Use * sections as tabs to glue box together.

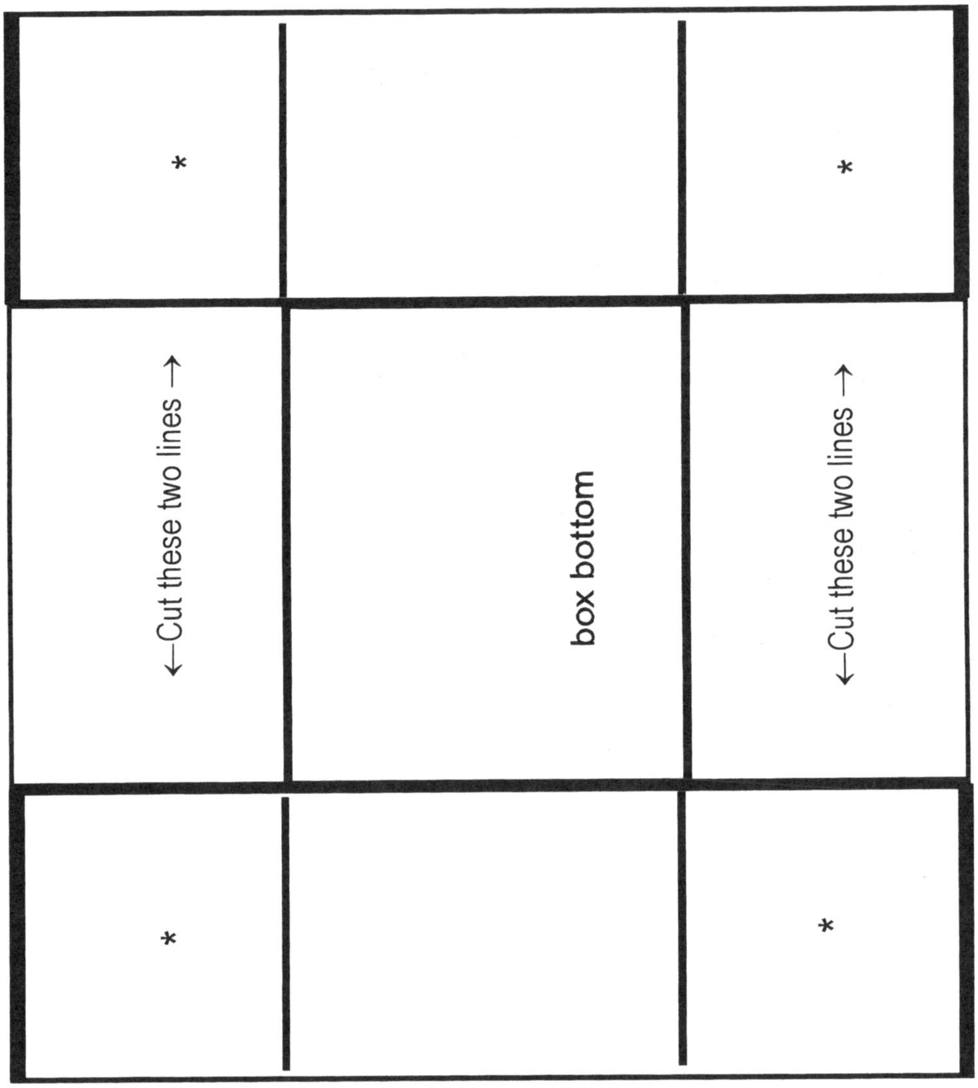

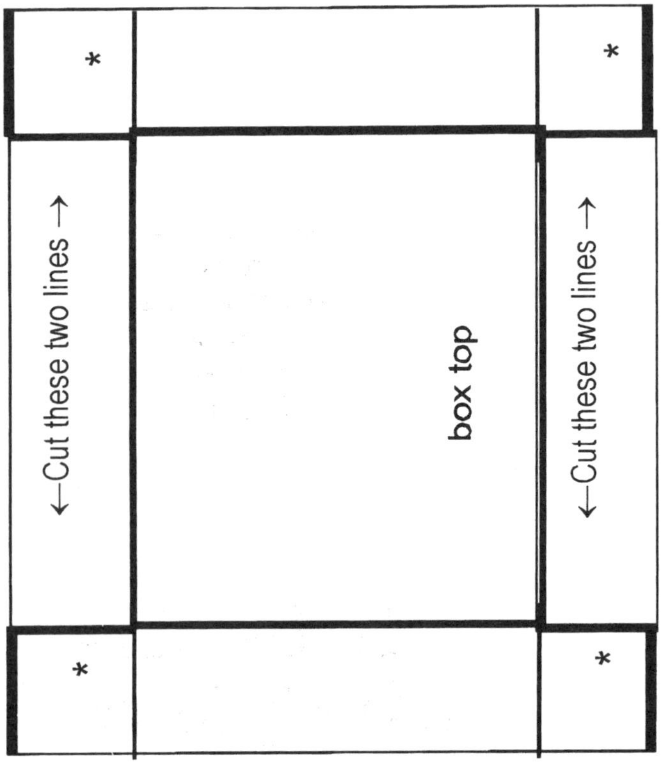

←Cut these two lines →

←Cut these two lines →

box bottom

box top

←Cut these two lines →

←Cut these two lines →

*

Thanksgiving Box

Students can add text and graphics to decorate top and bottom of box. Print, cut and fold to form small box for students to place handwritten "thanks" to remember in their prayers.

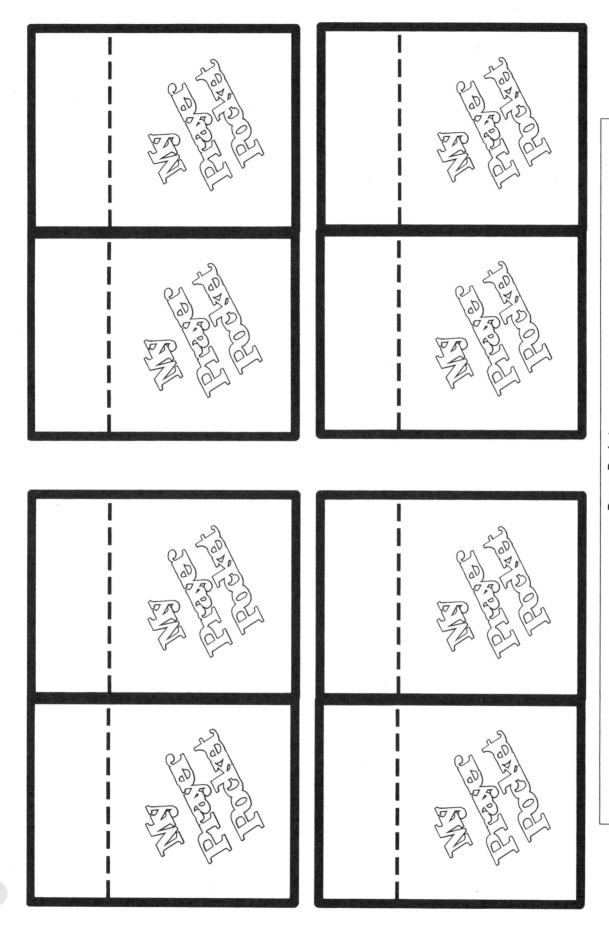

Prayer Pocket

Draw in Print Artist using basic shapes and lines. From the drop down menu choose Edit – select all. From the drop down menu choose Object – group. Save. Students can add text and graphics to personalize their own prayer pocket. Print, cut out and fold along center line. Glue together at open side and bottom being careful to place glue on edge only. Laminate for best results. Glue together at open side and bottom being careful to place glue on edge only. Laminate for best results. Encourage students to list prayer concerns on inside sheet, insert inside the prayer pocket and keep close at hand in pocket or purse.

Inside Sheets for Prayer Pocket

I will pray for:

I will pray for:

I will pray for:

I will pray for:

I will pray for:

I will pray for:

I will pray for:

I will pray for:

Page 2

Page 4

(This is the front)

(This is the back)

Page 3

Page 7

Page 8

Page 5

Page 6

Directions:
1. Fold and crease paper on all lines, making sure that all outside edges line up exactly.
2. Open sheet back to 8 ½ x 11 size.
3. Fold paper along solid line between pages 3 & 4 and 7 & 8. Cut paper along dotted line.
4. Fold page 4 to face page 5. Fold page 7 to face page 6. Press creases.
5. Open page (so that it measure 8 ½ x 11 again). Fold in half lengthwise so that cut opening is on top.
6. Pull solid center line (between pages 3 & 4) forward and crease.
7. Pull solid center line (between pages 7 & 8) back and crease.
8. Fold page 2 to face page 3, fold page 4 to face page 5, etc.

59

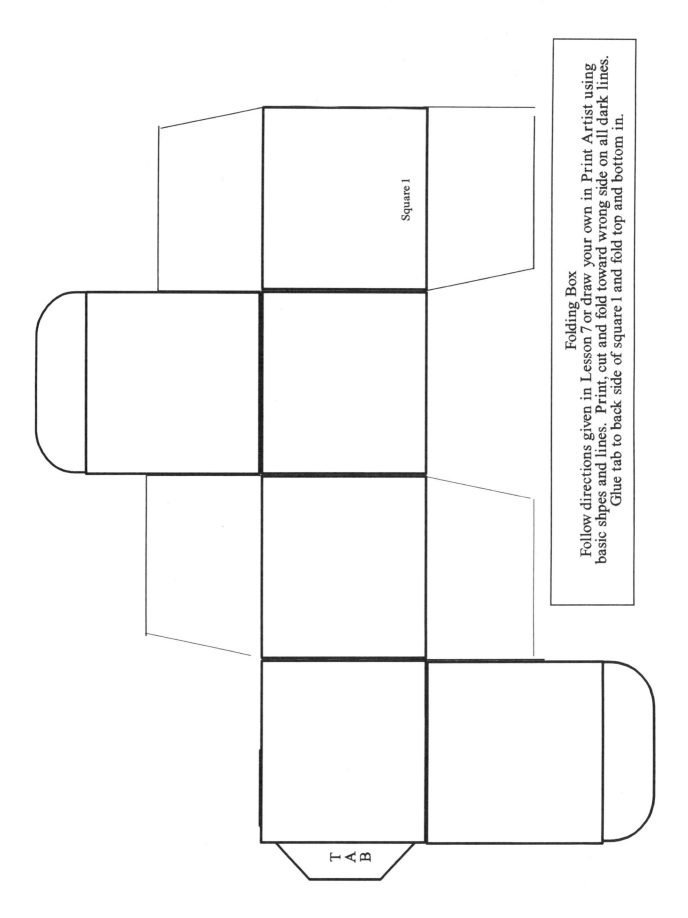

Square 1

Folding Box
Follow directions given in Lesson 7 or draw your own in Print Artist using
basic shpes and lines. Print, cut and fold toward wrong side on all dark lines.
Glue tab to back side of square 1 and fold top and bottom in.

T
A
B

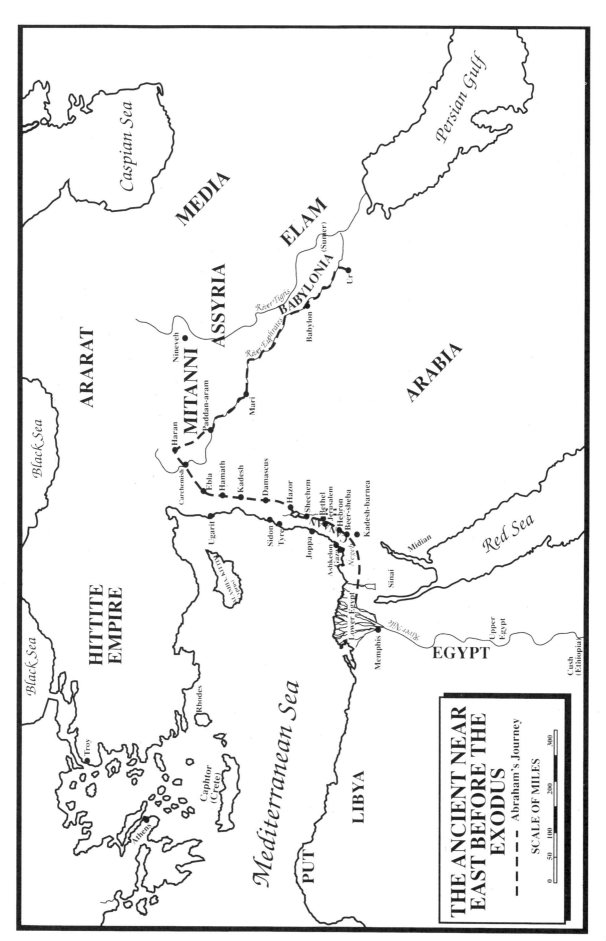

Caspian Sea

Persian Gulf

MEDIA

ELAM

ASSYRIA

BABYLONIA (Sumer)

River Tigris

River Euphrates

Nineveh

Babylon

• Ur

ARARAT

MITANNI

ARABIA

Haran

Paddan-aram

Mari

Black Sea

Carchemish

Ebla

Hamath

Kadesh

Damascus

Hazor

Shechem

Bethel

Jerusalem

Hebron

Beer-sheba

Kadesh-barnea

Ugarit

Sidon

Tyre

Joppa

Ashkelon

Gaza

Negeb

Midian

Red Sea

HITTITE EMPIRE

Rhodes

Troy

Caphtor (Crete)

Athens

Mediterranean Sea

Lower Egypt

Memphis

River Nile

Upper Egypt

EGYPT

Cush (Ethiopia)

PUT

LIBYA

THE ANCIENT NEAR EAST BEFORE THE EXODUS

- - - Abraham's Journey

SCALE OF MILES

0 50 100   200   300

Your Notes:

Your Notes:

Your Notes: